South W

Focus

To Stephanie and Jessica

South Wales in Focus

Barry Needle

foreword by Trevor Fishlock

seren

Seren is the book imprint of
Poetry Wales Press Ltd
Nolton Street, Bridgend, CF31 3BN, Wales
www.seren-books.com

First published 2000
© photographs Barry Needle, 2000
© introduction Trevor Fishlock, 2000

ISBN 1-85411-257-0

A CIP record for this title is available from
the British Library

The publisher works with the financial assistance of the
Arts Council of Wales

Printed in Perpetua by DWJ Colourprint, Port Talbot
Design and artwork: Simon Hicks

The great arm of land stretching westward from the gorges of the magisterial Wye to the promontories and skerries of Pembrokeshire seems to me unequalled anywhere. The landscape itself is a drama and there is barely an acre that cannot deliver a chapter of verse.

All of Wales is a marvellous mosaic of scenes and stories, and while many parts are wild, remote and scantily peopled, human experience has left no place truly barren. Along the southern coast and its hinterland the forces of geology and geography have fashioned a region of physical magnificence and charm, to which the beautiful photographs in this book bear full witness. The pictures also stimulate imagination, conveying the grandeur of the region's history, for southern Wales has borne its share of epics, and carries the scars of them. Anyone who travels the lanes and paths, hillsides, cliffs and beaches soon realises there is enough for half a dozen lifetimes of exploration.

In one way, I envy those who look upon the southern landscape for the first time. I recall the frisson of pleasure when I turned the corner and saw Three Cliffs Bay, sparkling in the Gower sunshine; the striking profile of Carreg Cennen Castle, grim above its unclimbable precipice; the roofless, evocative walls of Tintern beside the curving river; the exhilarating spectacle of peninsula Pembrokeshire's ramparts, locked in perpetual combat with the marching sea, the lovely falls at Ystradfellte. I remember the first of many ascents of Pen-y-fan, senior mountain of the Brecon Beacons, and its breathtaking summit reward.

There was, too, the different sensation of coming into the Rhondda for the first time, sensing its stubbornness and power and its century of tumult. And not only the Rhondda. Its sister valleys with their terrace rows of 'little palaces' drew me into their strong and sometimes poignant atmosphere and their resonances of a tremendous industrial, political and social epoch. Part of that story can be seen in Cardiff, where the City Hall lords it aldermanically over the Welsh Washington of Cathays Park, the heart of a capital made rich and famous by coal. The Pierhead Building tells of the heyday when Cardiff was one of the great ports of the world, despatching cargoes of energy to the earth's corners.

The way that the past is plaited into the landscape lies at the core of my enjoyment of it. It is not hard to imagine, for example, what sea air and light and the sense of space along the coast meant to miners and their families. The sea is there to ponder upon, and in the harbours and bays there are eloquent reminders that Wales has been a considerable seafaring nation. The lifeboat memorial at Port Eynon and the black bones of the *Helvetia* at Rhossili tell of the notorious force of gales and the risks that men took. Further along the coast, the treacherous Cefn Sidan sands trapped hundreds of sailing ships, and hundreds more were torn to splinters on the rocks of Pembrokeshire.

The sea borders of southern Wales are pitted with the tiny ports and smugglers' coves that have generated volumes of tales and legends. And there are resorts too, like the miners' favourite, cheery Porthcawl; and charming Tenby with its Georgian houses, its splendid beaches and its memories of bathing machines and modest dipping. In the sunlight it can often seem to the fanciful to be a fragment of the Mediterranean transported as a gift to Wales.

Whether on the coast or inland, you are rarely a mile or two from one of the numerous castles which speak of the spirit of resistance of the Welsh and their determination to endure; and also the determination of conquerors to keep them in order. Carew Castle, between Tenby and Pembroke, and Kidwelly Castle, which was built to control the crossings of the Gwendraeth rivers, were constructed to bring their districts of south Wales under Norman mastery. Kidwelly, though, was taken and re-taken by Welsh princes determined to fight back.

If Wales was comprehensively castled, it was also well-garrisoned by churches and chapels.

The nonconformist movement had its origins in Wales before the Civil War. In the centuries that followed, the Anglican church, largely favoured by the gentry, was powerfully challenged by the democratic and radical Welsh chapels.

The pictures in this book, the set-pieces, the unexpected and the sympathetic insights, are the product of a discerning eye. Each one reveals something of the remarkable variety and the many layers of this broad sweep of Wales. They amount to an inspiring invitation, leading the way into the story of a land observed with affection and respect.

Trevor Fishlock

Three Cliffs Bay, Gower

Kilvrough Woods, Parkmill, Gower

Three Cliffs Valley, Gower

Memorial to Lifeboatmen, Port Eynon

Worm's Head, Rhossili, Gower

Worm's Head Causeway

The *Helvetia* wreck, Rhossili

Rhossili Bay, Gower

Bracelet Bay, Mumbles, Swansea

Morriston Tabernacle Chapel, Swansea

Castle ruins, Swansea

Swansea to Cork Ferry

Swansea, looking east from Mayhill

M4, Junction 42 to Swansea

Hendy, near Pontarddulais

Swiss Valley Reservoir, Llanelli

Felinfoel, Llanelli

Shipwreck, Cefn Sidan, Carmarthen Bay

River Gwendraeth, Kidwelly

Kidwelly Castle

Carew Castle, Pembrokeshire

St. Florence, Pembrokeshire

Tenby Harbour

Lily Pond, Bosherston, near Pembroke

Broadhaven South, Bosherston

South Pembrokeshire Coast

South Pembrokeshire Coast

Stack Rocks, South Pembrokeshire

Stack Rocks, South Pembrokeshire

The Green Bridge of Wales, South Pembrokeshire

Pentre Ifan Cromlech, Preseli Mountains

Cynghordy Viaduct, near Llandovery

Carmarthen Fan viewed from Llanddeusant

Llyn y Fan, Carmarthenshire

Llyn y Fan

Bridge Street, Llandeilo

The Post Office, Trap, near Llandeilo

Carreg Cennen Castle, near Llandeilo

Carreg Cennen Castle and Black Mountain

Carreg Cennen Castle

Stream, Black Mountain

Henrhyd Waterfall, Coelbren, Dulais Valley

Lower Clun-Gwyn Falls, Ystradfellte

B.P. Plant, Baglan, Port Talbot

Port Talbot, looking west towards Swansea Bay

Port Talbot Steelworks from Baglan Top

Chapel Ruin, Margam, Port Talbot

Abbey Ruins, Margam

Pontrhydyfen, Afan Valley

Cymmer, Afan Valley

Number 8, Gelli Houses, Cymmer

The Bwlch Road into Rhondda, Cwmparc below

Craig y Llyn, near Hirwaun

Cwmparc, Rhondda

Stanleytown, Rhondda

Tylerstown, Rhondda

Stanleytown, Rhondda

Ferndale, Rhondda

Ferndale, Rhondda

A4061 at the head of the Ogmore Valley

The upper Ogmore Valley

Coney Beach, Porthcawl

Promenade and Pavilion, Porthcawl

Church Cottage, Merthyr Mawr, near Bridgend

Merthyr Mawr

The Dipping Bridge, Merthyr Mawr

Ogmore Castle, near Bridgend

Southerndown, near Bridgend

Dunraven Bay, Southerndown

Dunraven Bay, Southerndown

The Pierhead Building, Cardiff

City Hall, Cardiff

Castell Coch, near Cardiff

Caerphilly Castle

Fochrhiw, Rhymney Valley

Greenfield Terrace, Abercynon

Spencer Street, Cwmaman, near Aberdare

Six Bells, Abertillery

Six Bells, Abertillery

Penydarren, Merthyr Tydfil

Cefn Coed Viaduct, Merthyr Tydfil

Taf Fechan Stream, between Merthyr and Talybont

Sgwyd yr Eira Waterfall, near Penderyn

Foothills of the Brecon Beacons

Pen y Fan and Corn Ddu Peaks, Brecon Beacons

The summit of Pen y Fan

Cribyn viewed from Pen y Fan

On Cribyn

Corn Ddu, Brecon Beacons

Cantref, near Brecon

River Usk at Crickhowell

Across Clydach Gorge, near Brynmawr

On Blorenge, near Blaenavon, towards Sugar Loaf

River Usk, near Newport

Monmouthshire and Brecon Canal at Llanfoist

Raglan Castle, near Monmouth

River Wye at Bigsweir

River Wye at Tintern

Tintern Abbey

The River Wye near Chepstow

All photographs were taken using a tripod-mounted Mamiya C330 6x6cm twin lens reflex camera with 65mm, 80mm, 135mm, 180mm and 250mm lenses. Film was Fujichrome Velvia or Provia 100 (the latter preferred in bright sunlight for its greater tolerance of contrast). Extensive use was made of a polarising filter and occasionally an 85A warm-up.

Thanks to Mick Felton and his team for having the faith and vision to publish the book, to Trevor Fishlock for writing the Foreword, and to my wife Cheryl for her support and tolerance when I spent more time with my camera than I did with her.

Barry Needle

Barry Needle was born and bred in Port Talbot, South Wales.

He started his working life as an apprenticed fitter in the steelworks. After leaving the steel industry, he turned his hand to a variety of ventures, before settling in parcel distribution, where he works as an assistant depot manager. He now lives in Llanelli. Once a motorcycle racer, Barry now spends his spare time expanding his portfolio of photographs of the South Wales landscape. This is his first book.